Etsy Easy Guide:
Best Methods For Beginners On Making Money On Etsy

Table of content

Introduction

There are many businesses and business ideas that keep on coming online. A decade ago, there was little knowledge on affiliate marketing. Even though sales on commission, which is the mother of affiliate marketing already existed, affiliate marketing had not taken root in the internet world as it is today. The internet continues to experience the invention of brilliant business ideas which go a long way into making millions of dollars to people and companies behind such ideas. What many people look for is a good and a workable idea, which when established, they embrace and make money out of it.

A decade ago, a company called Etsy was started. At that time, those behind it never knew that their small idea would be driving millions of dollars online in form of sales ten years later. None of them had an idea that five years from their launch, they would be doing an initial public offer for their shares. That is the success of Etsy Company that runs the Etsy website. This pioneered the concept of Etsy business concept.

Over time, many people appreciated the idea which to date, is considered brilliant. That is why today, we have companies like **Three Bird nest**, **Simple Shapes**, **The black Apple**, **Matte Art**, **Christy Studio**, **College-O-rama**, and **Purple possom** among many others. Etsy business concept got established as a good business idea, and over the years, people have embraced it.

This is why as an individual, you need to understand the concept of Etsy business very well and join the millions of people in the business. Etsy sellers are today attaining financial independence. The process is so easy. It first of all needs understanding. You too can join today and be among those earning millions of cash.

Chapter 1: What is Etsy business?

How many of us understand the concept behind Etsy? It's good to understand it before going ahead to start it. This is very important as it helps in making a good and sound decision.

What is Etsy business?

Etsy as a business concept is based on peer to peer relationship where people focus on selling valuable and unique handmade products or supplies. The concept of etsy originated from the website *etsy.com* which pioneered this peer to peer website. People can sell many products or items from a wider range of industries so long as it's valuable and had existed for at least 20 years. Items that can be traded are from categories such as art, photography, clothing, jewelry, food, bath and beauty products among many others.

The opportunity for people to sell unique goods is so big and is yet to be untapped. If you imagine all the items people have in life and the technological advancement which has taken place in the past 20 years, you will have an idea of why those old items are considered valuable and are sought out for by many people.

Etsy business enables people from all walks of life to sell to one another valuable vintage items they have through online market places like *etsy.com*. When you look at Etsy business and its concept, you'll realize how people love outdated items which are no longer in the market in their old form. For example, you have seen people selling photos which were taken in 1970s. Such photos normally sell because they are highly valuable yet unavailable.

Now, Etsy business, as we have seen, entails different categories of items. Among the many categories available, people love photography. Most people also have a liking for jewelry, beauty products and so many things. This means you can look through these categories and find the one that suits or offer a unique preposition.

You can target certain geographical segment of the market with an idea of etsy business or just the global market. One thing with the global market is that there are so many hurdles you can face and even logistical nightmares. One of the challenges you will face is the language problem as there are some people who can't speak a word in English. There are also people with funny legislation, hence, can work hard and still sell to the wrong market.

Characteristics of an Etsy Business

If you want to run an Etsy business, it's good to know some of the characteristics thereof. This is important because the moment you decide to start an Etsy business, it enables you have a clear view of how an Etsy business ought to be run.

One characteristic of an Etsy business is that it's a peer to peer platform where two sets of people meet. The two sets of people are the users who register to order items and the users who register and list the vintage items for sale.

The second characteristic is the sale of the vintage items. Etsy business isn't just the sale of anything. It has to be an item which has existed for at least 20 years. This is the key thing that differentiates Etsy from any other business online. While many websites online sell the latest products and services, Etsy prides in selling those that are outdated. It's only special and valuable items that are kept for all that period of time.

The other characteristic is that there are two sets of people who meet though a platform. One group expresses the interest to buy the vintage items while the other sells the items. The platform charges the group that sells the vintage item a listing fee.

There are perhaps more characteristics of Etsy business. But even with the ones I've mentioned, you can point out an Etsy business opportunity and invest in.

Chapter two: The growth of Etsy business

This concept was not there before Etsy website was founded. Etsy website was founded in June 2005 by a small firm which was headed by Robert Kalin, Chris Maguire and Haim Schoppik. The website continued to develop as people continually joined the ownership and as investors also kept pumping more money into the business. This went on until its listing in the stock market in 2010. This became the birth of Etsy business concept.

After the inception of Etsy business and the success afterward, people realized how vintage items are greatly and highly valued. This can also be seen in international public auction where items for millions of dollars. So many businesses have since come up with online shops driven by Etsy business concept and are making pretty good money.

Some of the businesses which are doing so well with Etsy business include **Three Bird nest** which sells headbands, **simple shapes** selling vinyl graphics, **The black Apple**, **Matte Art**, **Christy Studio**, **College-O-rama** which sells pictures to be printed on books, and **Purple possom** which sells stickers for use on monthly photos of infants and toddlers, festive home decor and many others.

The idea in Etsy business is the vintage item. That's all that matters. Are you able to spot a vintage item with so much value? Provide a market place for such vintage items and allow members of the general public or the global society to list the amount of money they have, and sell to those interested.

Etsy businesses will continue to thrive even in years to come. Every passing day, an item becomes a vintage item because of age that passes. If you buy a bag for your child and keep it until the child joins high school, the bag becomes a vintage item. Others are such as photos of former president of a given country when he was probably in court or in prison. There are lots of items which, as days go, qualify to be vintage items.

Etsy business seems to be having a very bright ahead as many parties are likely to join the market. There are many chances for those interested. One of the reasons why chances are left open for those seeking to start Etsy business is so that there are more Etsy businesses online, which then will lead to stiff competition.

Secondly, a lot of industries out there haven't started the Etsy business and this leads to difficulty when it comes to penetrating the market. The third reason is, just like many other businesses, where there is competition you get the best of the competitors and consumers benefit. When you start an Etsy business, you will learn from your competitors, and this will collectively open the market wider, leading to more business opportunities.

Did you know that with Etsy business, someone can become a retailer while another becomes a wholesaler? This is another aspect of growth Etsy business has brought. People and businesses can actually come up with collection points and buy these items in bulk and supply. When dispatching the items to the end buyer, a wholesaler makes work much easier. So when you look at it, there is room for wholesalers, retails and distributors.

There is also business for the insurance firms that insure the items during transit. You can also find other opportunities such as repair and branding, created by this business concept. Businesses can come up to brand items before being placed in the market for sale. Transaction processing and payment gateway is yet another opportunity created by the Etsy business. If you offer a payment gateway like PayPal, Etsy business will make you salivate because you will need to connect more platforms to be able to offer or receive payments.

Regardless of how you look at it, Etsy business is here with us and as a result has re-energized so many businesses. You can look at all the aspects of Etsy businesses mentioned and see an opportunity that fits you. If you are a web developer, you can begin to think of how to come up with a platform where people interested in Etsy business can get content management system for the Etsy business. You can set yourself apart as Etsy business web development partner and those with interest in Etsy business will definitely come to you.

Chapter 3: How to start an Etsy Business

A good number of people have so far joined and are operating Etsy business. Just like any other business, it is something that needs prior planning. Just because the sellers make high sales does not mean that you will also have a smooth ride. There are a lot of things that come by it, which you need to keenly look into.

In this Chapter, I want to share with you some of the top tips you can give consideration to when you want to start an Etsy business. It is not an easy thing to start however, since there are lots of competitions here and there. For this reason, it takes one to be ready to soar in the challenges and aim at overcoming them. Many people started but have fallen off in the course of it, the difference between you and them is the effort and the determination you will purpose to make to ensure that you overcome all hurdles.

Tips to start an Etsy business

1. *Do a research*

Any successful business person, be it online or offline, carries out an extensive research about the products they want to sell before embarking on selling it. Carrying a research online when you want to start the Etsy business is very essential. It equips you with the kinds of things you can expect in the course of the business. Just because you make beautiful products and list them on Etsy isn't a guarantee that there will be influx of buyers willing to buy your products. Search, and also ask around to see whether there are other people selling the same products as yours, and see if they have market or not. This entails putting strategies in place. Wherever there is an appropriate strategy, success is inevitable. Some of the platforms which you can carry out the searches are Pinterest, Google searches, image searches, and even Etsy itself. You can also enquire from the Etsy sellers and get to know some of the pros and cons of the business.

2. Originality

Originality is the sense of being independent, creative and unusual. That you make a similar product as your competitor does not mean you cannot sell. There's a way you can make your product unique and original. Many people have won in the midst of stiff competition. What made them rise above their fellows is the sense of originality in terms of aspect, style and design. So when you want to start an Etsy business, first of all identify what makes your product different from the rest. This is solely to be able to attract the attention of the buyers, and make them leave all other products and settle on yours alone.

3. Target market

In the business world, there is always a target market. It is also the same thing with Etsy business. A target market is a person you envision when making a product or when coming up with a business idea. When you want to start an Etsy business, you need to think as a customer would think, especially when he/she is looking for a particular product. This will help you develop your shop's brand, hence will put you in a better position to cater for the needs of your customers appropriately. The needs can be in terms of age, sex and occupation.

4. How then can you think like a customer?

This is very easy. When you are creating your products, marketing them and even pricing them, make sure you 'put yourself in the mental shoes' of your prospective buyer. Also, find out some of the keywords they'll use to search for the products and find them easily. You can include other useful information such as the usage of the products and their expiry dates in the tags, titles and descriptions.

The truth is, when you identify your target market, you will be able to know the direction to take your business. This will also help you come up with strategies of expanding your product line at a given time.

5. Come up with a high quality photos

There's an old adage that says, 'first impression is the last impression'. This adage works well on Etsy business. Etsy is basically an image-driven website, and with this in mind, buyers decide quickly on what they see, based on the taste and preferences as well as the quality of products they see in your shop.

When you want to start an Etsy business, find ways through which the above adage can work for you. The secret is creating high quality photography. This, however, you do not need to do with an expensive camera. You can use a simple camera to creatively capture beautiful product images, which will guarantee you great success in your business.

Also, when capturing your products' images, be careful to capture even the background. Many shoppers love shopping in a clear, clean, clutter-free place as it provides an ideal environment for shopping.

6. Do appropriate pricing

There are so many sellers who, even with the greatest ideas they have about their businesses, they still end up making losses, not because of anything, but because of poor pricing they do to their products. With Etsy, you've got to be very careful when it comes to pricing. You might overprice or even underprice. When it comes to pricing, your foremost priority ought to be paying yourself first. And as you pay yourself for the product you've made, ensure it is a fair pay. Accurately count your cost, and do not underprice your items.

7. Network and advertise yourself

This should come immediately after you have researched and identified the target market for your products and now ready for action. It is when you spread news about the brand new business you are about to start.

There are several ways through which one can advertise himself. Some can be through the vintage methods such as following community members, while, you can also use the modern ways such as posting on blogs.

8. Time! Time! Time!

Time, as they say, is money. What amount of time are you willing to dedicate for your shop? Successful Etsy sellers will tell you that the success of their Etsy businesses comes as a result of the time they devote for their shops, regardless of the number of sales made.

First of all, one of the things you've got to put to consideration in order to succeed when you want to start an Etsy business is creating time as well as effort to look around for the kind of quality images that you will use to showcase the items for sale. One of the examples you can opt for is having an attractive, informative and friendly announcement for your shop. Others are such as having well written descriptions of items, short and catchy phrases as well as keywords for each listing. Also, spending your time to come up with your Etsy shop banners, descriptions, policies and terms of sale will go a long way towards attracting buyers, hence making high sales.

All these do not end there however. There is the element of running or managing a shop once it's created. This, in itself involves a whole lot of activities that really will require much of your time. Since Etsy business is operated online, you will have to regularly check in on the shop, check and answer conversations, change listings here and there, check the shop's traffic stats to see the number of visits people are making to the shop as well as responding to leads.

There are times when, you will have to severally go back to the drawing board until you finally grasp the winning idea. Time, just like most things in life, is related to success.

Therefore, before starting an Etsy shop, be ready to invest much of your time in order to realize success.

9. Have patience

Last, but not least, practice some patience. Any Etsy seller knows so well that success in Etsy busy does not come overnight. There are those who will not make any sale up to three months or so. It is after this period of time that they receive first order of items. This however does not mean that your products are not beautiful enough to be loved by customers or that your shop isn't worth visiting.

When in that period of waiting, you can look around for new things that can help market your products. Some of these include reading blogs of successful business people. This will help you get new ideas on how to make sales, through unique ways such as adding new items, keywords and changing listings regularly.

Normally, it is in such times that many people throw in the towel and decide to close down their shops. As for you, just have it in mind that success comes with lots of patience.

With all the above illustrations, it tells how easy it is for you to start an Etsy business. It only takes your effort, determination and time, and above all, the positive mindset and you will be good to start.

Chapter 4: Key things to note about Etsy business

Knowing the tips and guidelines of how to start an Etsy business isn't just enough. There are a lot of things that you still need to know before you venture into the business. Many Etsy sellers are today enjoying their businesses, just because they employed these simple yet very effective strategies, which have to date enabled them achieve top success in their businesses.

To help you understand some of these strategies, I have listed blow some of the key things to note about the Etsy business.

1. *Keywords*

We all know how optimization of website and product description for highly searched for keywords is very much important. Alongside this, Etsy sellers know that highly specific keywords work so well in Etsy business. A bigger percentage of consumers go into searching for their products needs first before making any purchases. For instance, instead of just searching for '*bracelet*', one would search for '*Bridesmaid bracelet*'.

In Etsy business, as some of the top sellers can confirm, the topmost thing that leads to success having a specific keywords.

2. *Take great photos*

Like I mentioned in the previous Chapter, first impression is the last impression. Mere photos of your products will not make any difference. Great photos on the other hand will go a long way towards helping you make more and more sales irrespective of whether you are a novice in Etsy business. Take the attractive, eye-catching and quality photos which will grab the attention of the buyers from the search results and will help your products not only be featured in Etsy but all over the internet also.

Having great photos is one of the superb ways of bringing your items to life. Since buyers cannot touch or see your products, the photos should be able to tell them all. Showing your buyers every detail they need to know about your products via the photos is great, in order for them to purchase.

To test this, you can do a clickability test on yourself. What does it entail? Clickability test means searching for your items and looking at other items on the page. If your photos will catch your attention, making you feel like clicking them, then you are on the right track. However, if they won't impress you, then it means you'll have to work on them to make them attractive to your eyes, as that is the same way they would be to other buyers.

3.   Sell great products

Selling what you love is the greatest reward you can give yourself. It is what keeps you motivated even when there are no sales, or even when you have limited amount of time for the business. Etsy business has many sellers, some of which sell similar products. This can really discourage you as you'd face great and stiff competition from your competitors. Selling great, unique and high quality products will however set you apart from the rest and make you realize high sales in your Etsy business.

To find fulfillment and love what you sell, you can read things like magazines and blogs, which will greatly inspire you. Through these platforms, you can get to know some of the trendy products that people love to buy and/or wear. You definitely wouldn't want to imitate someone else's product, but just by looking around and being able to identify the difference thereof, will greatly inspire you to come up with great ideas about your products, thereby increasing your sales.

Together with this, you can also carry out research in and around Etsy and see what other sellers are selling. This will help you identify any product that only a few people or none is selling, and by coming up with it, you will be selling a product that sets you apart from the crowd. Take your time and look in the various categories and subcategories and see what will make you stand out from the rest.

4.   Be found in Search

This is another key thing that anyone willing to start an Etsy business ought to bear in mind. When you are in the Search, you will find yourself plus your product relevant to the needs of your prospective buyers. However, when you operate blindly, you will miss out on many things.

One of the things you can do is to get to know your buyers' needs. This you can do by finding out what they are searching for. Simply type what you sell in the search bar, and a list of the recent searches will appear. These are the recent customer search terms.

You also can improve your chances of making high sales by employing things such as using your tag spaces well, opting for specific keywords and eye-catching phrases that buyers will automatically search for. Also add several catchy, accurate descriptive terms in your titles. If you do this accurately, you can be sure to make high sales in the Etsy business, regardless of whether you are just a newbie or have stayed long in the business.

5.   Ship internationally

You may be wondering what importance this adds to your business. Etsy, as I mentioned in the beginning, was formed for the purpose of connecting people around the globe. When you sell just within your country, you are limiting your chance of making sales.

According to top Etsy sellers, a bigger chunk of Etsy's transaction is normally between a buyer and a seller from totally different countries. By selling all around the globe, you give yourself more chances of meeting many buyers from different countries.

Now, for people in the other countries to find you, you must be noticed in the searches made by people from other countries, and the only way to achieve this is by shipping your products to other countries. So this will enable you to not only sell to buyers in your country, but also to others from other countries.

Chapter 5: Strategies of operating a successful Etsy business

Just like any other business, opening an Etsy shop is just one of the successes. There is however a whole lot of things that you should work on, such as the attention to the fine details of the business, giving considerations to the customers' needs and so many other things that come by. All these are to make you stand out from your competitors.

Below are some essential tips and secrets I want to share with you that will help you operate a successful business on Etsy. These tips can work for you whether you are a beginner or not.

1.   *Carry out a market research*
Carrying out a market research to know your target market is very vital when it comes to selling online. The essence of carrying out this research is to give you the understanding that your shop doesn't exist alone. It exists in the midst of many other top selling shops in the Etsy business. Before you set up the business, it would be proper to give some thorough attention to some of the shops you like buying your personal items from. Get to learn from them what they do that sets them apart from other sellers. You also can consider giving attention to your competitors as well as some other sellers who sell products as your own. Carrying out a market research will also help you be able to know the kind of products to sell depending on the target market available.

2.   *Identify yourself with the community*
Being a part of the great Etsy community will go a way towards helping you operate a successful Etsy business. You can provide valuable information as well as feedback, and also actively participate on the site's forum. It is also in the Etsy's community that you will reach out to some of the top sellers you have identified and seek their advice. When you also promote other sellers' products, you can be sure that yours too will be

promoted, and with this, you will be on your path to operating a successful Etsy business.

3.   Consider applying SEO

You could be wondering why some Etsy sellers are really making it and are even registering high traffic stats. The answer is very simple. They understand that a greater chunk of their buyers come via the Web searches. For this reason, they spend most of their time ensuring that their Etsy shops are well set for great Search Engine Optimization (SEO). Carrying out tests such as A/B tests for your descriptions will help you write descriptions that will perfectly go well with the needs of your customers. Such tests also help you optimize your listings.

Since search engines also give inbound links from other trusted sites to your shop great priority, you also can consider starting your blog or even contributing to other blogs and also seek reviews from your customers about your products as this will also provide links to your shop. In all these, remember you are seeking to extend your reach. Another thing that will also help with search engine results is regularly updating your shop.

4.   Establish and maintain a good rapport with your customers

Excellent customer service is never an easy thing, nevertheless, it is always a keynote component to an unending success. Similar to how you present your products, how you present yourself matters a lot to the prospective buyers. This is portrayed in the way you respond to your customers' concerns. Reply promptly to questions and feedback from your client, as you also respond generously to any problem they might have. This will not only help you build trust between you and your potential buyers but will also help you build repeat business. As a result of your great and commendable customer relations, your satisfied and thrilled customers will go an extra mile to recommend your shop to their friends, with whom you also can establish a lasting rapport.

5. Great, killer photographs and detailed descriptions

Pictures, as they say, speak volume of words. This becomes more than just a statement with Etsy business, whose transactions are done online. It is so amazing that Etsy buyers shell out money for products they haven't seen or touched, or even had chance to try on. This means that photographs and the descriptions really need to be up-to-the-minute.

When taking the photos, always ensure that they are taken professionally, with vivacious colors and in a way that makes them conspicuous. Make sure that you have a good camera that will bring out your products in a good way. High quality photographs give signals to the buyers that you are a trusted seller who cares so much about what he/she presents to the buyers.

Chapter 6: Attaining financial independence with Etsy business

There is nothing as beautiful as being financially independent. Many people desire to be financially independent in their entire lives. With Etsy, you can be sure to attain financial independence even if you are just a beginner. You do not need to be a long time seller at Etsy to be independent financially.

When you follow the above Sub-topics keenly and with determination, then you can be sure to attain financial independence in the end.

Etsy business is highly beneficial more than one's own site. With it, you can earn so much cash since it has lots of traffic, and its listings also show up high in the Google ranks. These, when translated to sales, can earn you so much cash, which then gives you the financial freedom.

Chapter 7: Conclusion- it is real and works!

It is evident that whether a beginner or not, you can start an Etsy business and successfully attain financial independence, which everyone else wants in life.

Many people who probably tried the Etsy business but failed have risen up to give wrong and misleading information about it. This however should not discourage you if you are determined to start up the business. Etsy is real and works, and within no time, you will be counted among the world's prominent millionaires!

Try it today!

www.ingramcontent.com/pod-product-compliance
Lightning Source LLC
Chambersburg PA
CBHW071204220526
45468CB00003B/1154